••• Consider it

Pure Joy...

An Introduction to Clinical Trials

By Ann Raven

Consider it .... *ver*
you f(....

(James 1, v2)

For Luke

First published 1991
2nd Edition 1993
This third edition published 1997 by
Cambridge Healthcare Research Ltd ©

ISBN 0 9517396 1 1 "Consider It Pure Joy..."

Designed by Insight Graphic Design/Leverpress of Ipswich.

Foreword

It is always easier to do something which one enjoys. Certainly this applies to clinical research conducted to the standards that are now expected. It would, however, be unrealistic to expect the discipline of clinical research to be anything other than tough. Where a trial has gone well, and the investigators and all the others involved have demonstrably done their very best, then the 'feel-good' factor for a job well done is just reward. When a trial has not been straightforward, and there have been problems, the pleasure of completion may be muted, though tempered by the success of having overcome the difficulties.

Ann Raven has been providing guidance and wisdom in this field for many years now, and those who were familiar with this book in its previous edition will be very pleased to see it reappear, so that others can derive the information and pleasure from it, in a research context, that they did. Many of the guidelines on various aspects of clinical research have changed over the years. Common sense, as exemplified in this book, has not, and the purpose of the previous edition in providing valuable information which is strictly practical, easy to read and therefore likely to be remembered is again served. There is a new section on pharmaco-economics which reflects the importance given to this subject both inside and outside the research-based pharmaceutical industry at the present time, and this section, which explains the relevance of quality-of-life studies as well as the strictly economic arguments, adds to the value of the book.

Research can be fun as well as hard work. The reader of this book is likely to find both, and will derive a great deal of enjoyment from absorbing and putting into practice what it says.

Dr Frank Wells
Director, Medical Affairs, ABPI

Preface to the Third Edition

Successful clinical drug development relies on the united endeavours of a multitude of people. Some are rather visible: doctors and patients and the senior medical executives of the Pharmaceutical Industry. There is a plethora of sophisticated textbooks for the physicians and scientists, and complex guidelines abound. This book is written for the unsung heroes, whose names seldom appear on publications and who may never visit the research centres, but whose role is vital. There is now a vast army of administrative and technical staff who work in offices, libraries, laboratories, data management departments and pharmacies and who support this complex process.

For all those who are new to the job and for whom the jargon of clinical trials is something of a mystery, I have tried to present a brief introduction to the process and to explain and define some of the expressions employed.

The first edition was produced primarily for my own support staff in a large clinical trials department, but I was encouraged to publish it. It has since been used as the basis of training and induction courses in the Drug Industry in Europe and the USA, to provide career guidance for those aspiring to join the Industry and also in medical schools. I am delighted that it has proved useful to a wider audience and that continued sales have justified the production of this revised third edition.

Ann Raven : January 1997

ACKNOWLEDGEMENTS
I would like to acknowledge the support and encouragement of many friends and colleagues in the Industry, especially those who have made helpful suggestions for this new edition. Also the patience and skills of Juliet Corfield who prepared the manuscript.

Contents

CHAPTER 1   # Drug Development

How are new drugs discovered?

Drugs have been in use for thousands of years and come from many and various sources. They include plant and animal extracts, antibiotics from micro-organisms and an assortment of synthetic chemical compounds. Today there are about a thousand medicinal compounds in common use, most of which have been developed from a few dozen 'prototypes'.

Early pharmaceuticals were natural products and derivatives, such as aspirin from willow bark and penicillin from moulds. Plant extracts have lost much of their popularity in this century since the majority are much more toxic than their synthetic equivalents and only very few new drugs have been discovered from this source in the last 50 years.

A significant advance in drug research was the discovery of organ extracts and hormones. For example, the lives of millions of diabetic patients were saved following the isolation of insulin in 1921. Many other drugs were discovered through an improved understanding of enzymes and receptor sites in the early 1960s, for example the beta blockers used in heart disease, anti-inflammatory drugs used to relieve arthritis and anti-ulcer drugs. More recently genetic engineering and advances in cell biology and biotechnology have led to the discovery of many exciting products, bringing cures or relief to groups of patients who, hitherto, had no therapies available.

Following discovery and production of a **New Chemical Entity (NCE),** drug development tends to follow a pattern. This now involves the use of laboratory and animal experiments, as required by government regulations. Pharmacologists have developed sophisticated screening tests to help them recognise promising new drugs. These tests usually involve inducing the target symptom or disease in laboratory animals and then studying the effect of the new compound. The development of such **animal models** has done much to improve our understanding of both the disease processes and new treatments, for animals and man.

When a promising compound emerges from screening the chemists often produce **analogues** - compounds with a very similar chemical structure. These also enter the screening programme in the hope that one or more of the series will be both safe and effective.

This rational approach has been greatly enhanced by the combination of chance and judgement known as serendipity. Many of our most successful drugs used today were identified as a result of chance observations during the search for something quite different.

What happens before drugs are tested on people?

In the 20th century, people have come to expect and demand high levels of safety and an almost complete lack of **toxicity** (literally, poisoning) for the ever increasing variety of drugs they consume. Whilst some drugs (particularly plant extracts) produce adverse effects immediately, many appear to be perfectly safe until they are taken over a long time. Therefore, once a prospective new drug has demonstrated a specific and interesting activity in the animal model, they must be subjected to a battery of toxicity tests in animals before they can be given to man.

In Europe it is normal practice to perform acute and chronic toxicity testing in a rodent species, e.g. rat/mouse, and a non-rodent, e.g. rabbit or dog. In the US three different species must be tested. Trained technicians observe the effects on the animals firstly using single doses of the test drug and later using repeated doses. Both sexes of animals of various ages are studied. Following the test period those animals which are sacrificed are examined minutely.

The objectives of these tests are to establish what **adverse effects** or toxicity occurs and at what dose. For instance, some drugs will cause liver damage, but only at high doses. In addition to normal toxicity testing, the effects of a new drug on fertility (reproductive toxicity) and on the foetus must be established (**teratology** tests). Long term safety and **carcinogenicity** tests in animals are conducted once the drug is approved for testing in patients.

Rigorous guidelines for these tests are provided by **regulatory authorities** relating to the species and numbers of animals, duration of testing and doses to be employed - relative to the intended use in humans.

Whilst animal toxicity tests are being conducted, many other activities take place which are also important for the drug development process - see fig 1. Production chemists will be developing manufacturing methods, others will be exploring different pharmaceutical formulations and conducting tests to find out how stable the drug is, at room temperature and in other conditions. More detailed **pharmacology** testing will be underway to establish not only the likely benefits in man but also potential side effects. Later, studies will be conducted to investigate whether the new drug interacts with other drugs, when taken at the same time. Metabolic tests which show how the drug is absorbed, distributed around the body and then broken down and excreted, will be conducted in animals. Pharmacokinetic studies are then conducted in animals and later in human volunteers. These measure the rate at which the drugs are absorbed, enter the blood system and are metabolised (or broken down and excreted). Results from all these pharmacology studies may provide useful indicators of future efficacy and safety in patients.

About the time that the drug is first tested on humans, the manufacturing process is **scaled up** and commercial sized batches of the newly formulated drug begin production.

It is estimated that only one in seven thousand

A Simplified Scheme Of New Drug Development

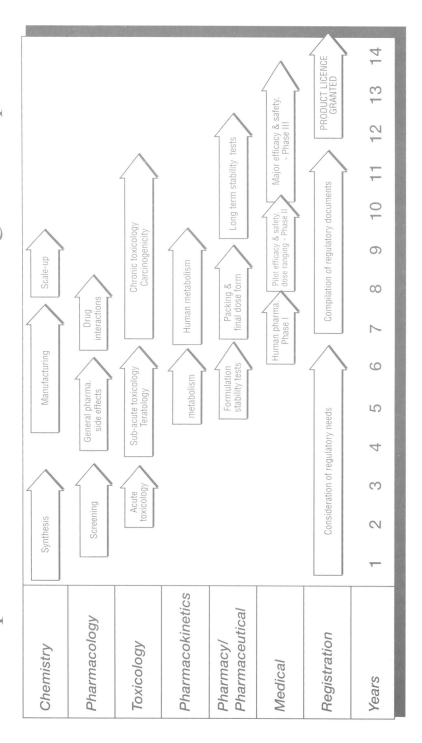

Chemistry	Synthesis	Manufacturing	Scale-up

| Pharmacology | Screening | General pharma. side effects | Drug interactions |

| Toxicology | Acute toxicology | Sub-acute toxicology Teratology | Chronic toxicology Carcinogenicity |

| Pharmacokinetics | metabolism | Human metabolism |

| Pharmacy/ Pharmaceutical | Formulation stability tests | Packing & final dose form | Long term stability tests |

| Medical | | Human pharma. Phase I | Pilot efficacy & safety, dose ranging - Phase II | Major efficacy & safety, - Phase III |

| Registration | Consideration of regulatory needs | Compilation of regulatory documents | PRODUCT LICENCE GRANTED |

| Years | 1 2 3 4 5 6 7 8 9 10 11 12 13 14 |

compounds, selected for further development after initial screening, progresses to a Product Licence in man. Most compounds are rejected in the acute toxicity testing process.

Why do human volunteer trials?

For most new drugs, it is considered preferable to conduct tests in healthy human volunteers before exposing 'sick' patients to them. Unlike the US and some other European countries, at present it is not necessary to obtain permission for volunteer trials from the regulatory authority in the UK. However, these trials, like those in patients, must be approved by an independent ethics committee.

Volunteer trials, also called **Phase I** trials, establish how the human body handles the new drug and what toxic effects, if any, are experienced. First, single doses are given, in slowly increasing quantities and then, if all appears to be well, repeated doses are given to different individuals. These trials are invariably **placebo-controlled** and involve only very limited numbers of healthy volunteers. Phase I trials are conducted in hospitals or commercial Human Pharmacology Units, where specialist medical attention could be immediately available if a serious adverse event occurred. Volunteers are monitored with extreme care throughout the trial. They are often drug company employees or medical students - traditionally, healthy young men who are paid for their involvement. Recent legislation also now demands that new drugs intended for an elderly population must also be tested in 'healthy' elderly volunteers. There are some drugs, such as chemotherapy agents used in cancer treatment, which could not be tested ethically in healthy volunteers. These special categories of drugs are tested only on selected 'patient volunteers' in hospitals.

How are drugs tested in patients?

Following Phase I trials in healthy volunteers, clinical trials in patients are divided into a number of further phases:

Phase II describes the first patient trials: these will be very carefully controlled trials aiming to give an idea of efficacy, which dose is optimal and some preliminary information on safety. This phase will usually involve only a few hundred patients. Some of the trials are likely to be placebo-controlled and frequently they are conducted in hospitals. If the results from Phase II are sufficiently promising and all the other drug development process is progressing smoothly, the drug company may decide to embark on the more expensive Phase III.

Phase III trials comprise the major efficacy and safety trials, often involving thousands of patients. Most of these trials will be conducted under the same conditions as would prevail once the drug was marketed, but with closer monitoring. Many Phase III trials are conducted therefore in general practice. This phase will include comparative trials with marketed treatments and also placebo-controlled trials. The results of the Phase III trials will be required before an application for a Product Licence can be submitted.

Phase IV trials are those performed after a drug has received a Product Licence and is marketed. Many questions may remain unanswered, such as effectiveness and safety in children or the elderly. Large Post Marketing Surveillance (**PMS**) studies are now often conducted on new drugs to identify rare adverse events. These also serve to establish the general usefulness of a new drug used in normal clinical practice in a significant number of patients.

Named patient treatment is a mechanism wherein an unlicensed drug can be supplied to a doctor for the treatment of a particular (named) patient. Drug companies are usually sympathetic to these requests, particularly where no alternative therapy is available, but the patient must be carefully monitored and a report submitted to the company.

Regulation of Drug Research

CHAPTER 2

Who makes the rules?

Before new drugs can be administered to patients in clinical trials, approval must, by law, be sought from the national regulatory authority.

In most countries, a panel of scientists employed by the national government reviews the available data and decides whether to grant permission for specific clinical trials to proceed. In some countries the company or individual researcher simply has to notify the government of their intentions.

In the US, the regulatory authority is known as the **FDA** (Food & Drug Administration) and clinical trials must be registered with this body via a Notice of Claimed Investigational Exemption for a New Drug (**IND**) which lays down the purpose and conduct of each trial.

In the UK, since the 1968 Medicines Act, there has been a comprehensive system of drug licensing which is handled by the Department of Health. The licensing authority can issue Product Licences, Manufacturers' Licences and Clinical Trial Certificates (**CTC**). There are a number of advisory committees consisting of independent experts including the Committee on Safety of Medicines (**CSM**) which advise on safety, efficacy and quality of new medicines. A sub-committee of the CSM investigates adverse event reports. Clinical trials in patients must be covered by a Clinical Trial Certificate or a Product Licence (**PL**), but since 1981 most trials have been conducted under the Clinical Trial Certificate Exemption (**CTX**) scheme. Under this scheme only a summary of the pre-clinical data and the trial protocol are submitted to the Medicines Control Agency (**MCA**). If the expert assessors find the data acceptable they will grant a CTX within 35 days. If the CTX submission is rejected, the company must apply for a full CTC which may take many months.

In the early '90s, the EC Commission set up a Committee for Proprietary Medicinal Products (**CPMP**) in Brussels which developed a system of mutual recognition between member states to reduce the duplication of evaluation of PL data. Now there is a European Medicines Evaluation Agency (**EMEA**) based in London and there are both centralised and decentralised procedures for product authorisation. Centralised procedures lead to Community Authorisation valid in all member states and the decentralised procedure is based on the Multistate system.

How are the drugs assessed?

Teams of expert assessors which include pharmacists, toxicologists, pharmacologists and clinicians review all the **pre-clinical** data and decide if the drug is safe to be given to patients - before a CTC, CTX or IND equivalent is granted.

During the clinical trial annual progress reports are usually submitted and all serious adverse events must be reported. When clinical development is completed a huge dossier containing all the pre-clinical, clinical efficacy and safety data, together with a number of **expert reports**, is compiled and submitted for a Product Licence. Evidence that the clinical research has been conducted to GCP standards is also submitted (see Chapter 3). The review process may take between 6 - 30 months for a Product Licence Application, depending on the country, type of drug and procedure involved.

What about ethics?

In addition to scientific review of information on the drug, clinical trials are subject to various ethical controls.

The Declaration of Helsinki is almost universally accepted as the standard code of ethics on human experimentation, encompassing research on both volunteers and patients. Whilst accepting that progress in medicine requires experimenting on humans, this document describes basic ethical principles including the requirement to obtain informed consent from each subject and an obligation to submit the **protocol** to an independent ethics committee for comment and guidance.

Most hospitals and Health Authorities in the UK have an ethics committee which consists primarily, but not exclusively, of medical staff. In some countries there are regional and even national ethics committees. Their composition and conduct is governed by slightly different guidelines in each country. In the UK there are several guidelines, including those published by the Department of Health and also the Royal College of Physicians. Protocols, together with often comprehensive proforma, are submitted by researchers for review at regular (usually monthly) meetings. The main objectives are to review trial protocols to ensure firstly that the trial is well designed and justified from the data available, and secondly that the risk to patients is minimal. Local ethics committees will also consider whether the facilities or staffing levels at the hospital or clinic are adequate for the proposed trial.

Obtaining ethics committee approval for multicentre trials can be a complex procedure as the investigator in each centre usually needs to submit the protocol to their local ethics committee, often with different requirements for proforma, documentation and administrative fees. The Royal College of General Practitioners Ethics Committee in the UK will review multicentre protocols for studies in general practice.

In the UK, if any ethics committee rejects proposals for a clinical trial, the regulatory authority should be notified. In many European countries, regulatory authorities consider the opinion of the ethics committee before giving their permission to conduct the trial.

Since ethics is not an absolute subject, there is much controversy about what should be permitted. You can imagine that the use of placebos in severely ill patients will be unacceptable to many. Conducting studies on children, the mentally ill or pregnant women also present particular ethical problems.

What is informed consent?

Patients who are invited to participate in clinical trials should be provided with adequate information about the trial before making their decision. Usually it is the doctor who will explain the reason for the trial, potential risks and benefits, briefly what is known about the test drug(s) and what measurements and procedures are involved. Absolute confidentiality in the trial report should be assured, although permission may be sought for the drug company medical department staff to review the patient's notes. The patients should be told that involvement is purely voluntary and that they are free to change their mind and withdraw from the trial at any time. Normally the patient is given this information in writing too and then should be allowed sufficient time to ask any questions and consider their decision.

Patients should not be offered any inducement to participate in a clinical trial and may not be paid, although travelling expenses may be offered, if appropriate, and trial drugs should be provided free of charge.

If the patients understand the implications and agree to participate, they are usually asked to sign a Consent Form, which is kept in their medical notes.

Good Clinical Practice

CHAPTER 3

What is Good Clinical Practice?

Originally Good Clinical Practice (**GCP**) was a set of proposals prepared and published in 1977 for the guidance of **investigators** and drug companies undertaking clinical trials in the US. They were prepared as a response to anxieties about the quality and reliability of some of the research data submitted to the regulatory authorities. Similar guidance also exists for Good Manufacturing Practice (**GMP**) and Good Laboratory Practice (**GLP**).

The main tenets of the GCP proposals are that clinical trials should be good science, verifiable, monitored, well documented and comply with high ethical standards. Although not initially popular even in the country of origin, GCP has now been accepted by drug companies and is the required standard for drug development aimed at international product licences. Some European investigators found the initial guidance rather unacceptable, but in 1991 an EC working party published European GCP guidelines and these are now being widely implemented. More recently the International Conference on Harmonisation (**ICH**) has achieved a harmonisation of the GCP guidelines developed in Japan, US and Europe and the resultant ICH GCP guidelines are now available. A copy can be obtained from the ICH Secretariat (address in Appendix) or via the Internet.

The subjects encompassed by the GCP guidelines are:
❏ the selection of investigators
❏ protocol content
❏ ethics committees and informed consent
❏ trial monitoring, data validation and source data verification
❏ adverse event reporting
❏ drug accountability
❏ data handling, use of computers and statistical analysis

❑ content of trial reports and investigator brochures
❑ standard operating procedures (**SOPs**) and quality assurance
❑ archiving **CRFs** and trial documentation

They are primarily organised under headings of **Sponsor** (drug company) Investigator and Ethics Committee responsibilities. One common theme throughout can be simplified as 'write down your procedures, then document what you do and be prepared for inspection'.

Why is GCP necessary?

Developing drugs is an expensive and lengthy business. (It may cost £100 million over more than 12 years to develop one licensed drug) and it is undesirable to repeat the process in different parts of the world. It is therefore a sound idea to ensure that the research data is acceptable to all national regulatory authorities. Since the US is the largest single market for pharmaceuticals, most drug companies wish to be successful there. The FDA will review clinical trial data only if it is conducted to GCP standards. The implementation of GCP guidelines is doubtless improving the quality of clinical trials sponsored by drug companies, and the harmonised approach is a major advantage for an international industry.

What difference does it make?

As companies implement the GCP guidelines they realise that there is a high price to pay for increasing standards - more staff are needed, each co-ordinating fewer trials with greater care. Clinical trials need not take any longer - and with more care about trial design and selecting investigators they could proceed more quickly - but there has been about a three-fold increase in the number of monitoring and secretarial support staff needed. In addition, SOPs must be written and a GCP Quality Assurance department established to conduct internal audits.

Not all staff take kindly to following SOPs or being

audited, so training and compliance programmes need to be established, even in the smallest companies. More documentation means more filing and archiving, leading to storage problems in some departments.

Finally, an important difference should be the confidence with which everyone can view the results of a clinical trial which complies with GCP, and the satisfaction of passing a stringent **audit** should not be underestimated!

CHAPTER 4

Clinical Investigators

Who are investigators?

On first hearing this expression you may think that this term refers to a kind of medical CIA! In fact, it is simply what the drug industry calls those who 'investigate' new treatments in patients. Invariably they are doctors who are sufficiently senior to have their own patients - in the UK this means a General Practitioner in the community or a consultant in a hospital. The senior person at any 'investigating' centre is termed the Principal Investigator and he or she may delegate much of the work to 'co-investigators', often junior doctors or research nurses and pharmacists. The principal investigator, however, retains legal responsibility. Sometimes in trials conducted in many sites (**multicentre trials**) there is an overall principal or co-ordinating investigator who may have a major role in designing the study, recommending other clinical investigators, interpreting and publishing the results.

Where do they work?

Investigators may work in any setting providing they have access to a suitable group of patients and facilities for examining and assessing them. Early studies with a new drug are normally conducted by investigators based in a teaching hospital. Larger studies are more frequently done in district general hospitals - with either in- or out-patients, depending on the disease and the drug. Recently, in the UK, there has been an increased emphasis on patients being managed in primary care rather than in hospitals. As a result of this there are now improved facilities in health centres and many more drug trials are now being conducted in the community. Health Care systems vary considerably throughout Europe, but everywhere the trend is towards an increase in Phase III trials in the primary health care setting.

How does a Sponsor find an investigator?

Finding the ideal investigator to conduct the trial is one of the greatest challenges for clinical trial staff. You need to find someone with considerable medical skill, commitment to research, good facilities, willingness to fill in endless forms and finally, access to lots of patients who trust him/her and who will consent to enrol in clinical trials. The most obvious approach is to speak to previous contacts and friends in the speciality and ask their advice. Anyone publishing a paper in one of the specialist medical journals is likely to be quite informed and motivated in that field, so a literature search can be fruitful (doctors who start trials but never finish them don't usually publish). Some investigators are identified at conferences - every speciality has it's own society and meetings. The Medical Register includes all British registered doctors together with their qualifications. In addition, the Medical Directory, published annually, theoretically lists all British doctors alphabetically and also all hospitals by region. This two volume tome is a mine of useful information. Each doctor entry gives details of training, qualifications, memberships of societies, major publications, current and previous jobs. Hospital entries list all consultants by department. In addition, doctors are listed by town and village if you prefer to make a geographical selection. In the back pages you will find addresses and staff details of universities and post-graduate institutes. (It is not comprehensive, however, and occasionally someone's name is missing; this doesn't mean they have been 'struck off', it could be that they simply didn't return the entry form in time or are only very recently qualified.) Most countries have a similar register of medical practitioners.

Once suitable potential investigators have been identified, the drug company CRA (or medical advisor) will approach them to discuss a) whether they wish to participate in a clinical trial, and b) whether they and their facilities are acceptable to the company. Not every qualified clinician is a successful investigator and in recent years many companies and health authorities have had cause to compile a **blacklist** of doctors who have demonstrated an inability to conduct clinical trials correctly.

What are study site co-ordinators?

This is a role that has gained popularity in recent years. With the increasing demands both of paperwork and tight schedule adherence in sponsored clinical trials, investigators have recognised the need for additional administrative help. Study site co-ordinators are usually nurses or health service researchers who can take responsibility for the day to day management of the trial(s) at that site. Frequently they will be employed by the hospital or health centre but financed through the drug company, and some work as freelancers via an agency.

A study site co-ordinator may be involved in identifying and screening suitable patients, co-ordinating and recording trial assessments, arranging follow-up appointments and patient recall, and maintaining trial records. They may become a key contact for the patient and trial monitor and tend to be highly valued by Sponsor and investigator alike for improving the efficiency of the trial.

How do you "address" an investigator?

Like many professionals, doctors are rightly proud of their qualifications and therefore it is important to understand them and their job titles. A newly qualified British doctor has to complete a pre-registration year as a Houseman or House Officer. Later he or she is promoted to **SHO** (Senior House Officer). The next step is Registrar in a speciality and two or three years later, Senior Registrar (**SR**). For many doctors the final step is promotion from SR to Consultant and, once appointed, consultants rarely move. In university (teaching) hospitals, a lecturer is equivalent to an SR and a Senior Lecturer to a Consultant. The head of an academic department may be a Reader or a Professor. On occasions eminent doctors are awarded a "Personal

Chair", that is, one which was created solely for them and will not be passed on. On retirement, these are termed Emeritus Professors.

At registrar level, hospital doctors usually study for post-graduate qualifications from the appropriate Royal College, to obtain e.g. membership of the Royal College of Physicians (MRCP, UK), Fellowship of the Royal College of Surgeons (FRCS) and possibly a research doctorate (MD) in their chosen speciality. A surgeon in the UK, who is an FRCS, is entitled to be called Mr. (Miss or Mrs.) instead of Dr. and obstetricians in England and Wales also follow this practice. In Scotland obstetricians consider this to be Sassenach nonsense and retain Dr. throughout! General practitioners in the UK are likely to have completed a three-year post-graduate vocational training to become accredited and they can also take membership exams to join the Royal College of General Practitioners. However well qualified, only partners in a GP practice may have their own list of patients.

(The abbreviations and usage of common UK medical qualifications are included under Resource Material at the back of the book.)

Why become an investigator?

What motivates a doctor to add to his hectic and demanding lifestyle by getting involved in clinical trials? Providing there is definite motivation, perhaps the exact reason is unimportant, but it should be understood that it is rarely primarily for personal gain, either financial or in prestige. Drug trials for pharmaceutical registration are infinitely more tedious in respect of form filling than any research a doctor might design himself and rarely lead to publication. Sometimes the individual doctor has no opportunity to contribute to the design of drug company trials. However, consultants often consider trials to be good training or discipline for their juniors. The research grants may help to fund badly-needed equipment, an extra pair of hands in the clinic or even a trip to an academic meeting in an exotic location! Usually there is a genuine concern to be contributing to the search for better treatments. A complicated trial may assist with team building and improve staff morale in, for example, psychogeriatric wards. Some doctors are quite simply flattered to be approached to undertake research with a new and potentially exciting drug.

What is the investigator's role?

Without clinical investigators the drug industry couldn't develop drugs. The industry is, therefore, completely dependent on a group of professionals who are not accountable to them and who are ultimately a principal customer. Investigators are central to the whole concept of clinical trials. They have an important role in trial design, case record form design, obtaining ethics committee approval, selecting patients, obtaining consent and treating and assessing patients in a trial. They also bear legal and moral responsibility for each individual patient's welfare. They can be expected to supervise (or delegate) the dispensing and accounting of drug supplies. Investigators must complete and retain complex documentation for the drug company and report any undesirable effects in trial patients. The industry expects investigators not only to participate in clinical trials, but to adhere to schedules, recruitment rates and protocols which the Sponsor dictates. It all sounds extremely burdensome, but amazingly enough the majority of investigators are pleased to interact with the drug industry and are invariably and genuinely welcoming to clinical trials staff (**CRA**s and others) who visit them regularly. For many industry people working in clinical trials the great attraction of the job is the interest and pleasure in collaborating with healthcare professionals.

Trial Design and Protocols

CHAPTER 5

What is Trial Design?

Every clinical trial is an experiment which aims to improve our knowledge about a new treatment for patients. The question to be answered may be quite simply "does it work?" or "is it safe?". Usually doctors want to be more precise than this, so it is common to ask "is this new drug better than the old one, either in terms of treating the disease better or quicker, or in terms of the same benefits but with fewer side effects?". There are many different ways to test the risks and benefits of new treatments; the trick is to choose the design which gives you an answer to the question as quickly as possible and involves the minimum number of patients in the experiment. The design of the trial is a description of the way patients will be studied, in terms of selection, treatment and assessment.

How are trials designed?

Clinical trials may be designed by a medical advisor or clinical research associate (CRA) within a drug company R&D or medical department. Alternatively, the design may be proposed by a doctor or even a medical group who might then approach the drug company asking for supplies of a new drug treatment. However, a good design results from a multidisciplinary approach.

When drug company staff are involved, they are usually not specialists in every aspect of trial design, so they have to spend some time asking for advice and generally finding out how to proceed.

Questions which need to be asked are:
- ❑ What are the objectives?
- ❑ Which disease should be treated (this is sometimes called **the indication** for treatment)?
- ❑ What sort of patients might benefit?
  e.g. age, sex, duration and severity of illness

❏ How many patients do we need to study?
❏ Where are those patients normally treated?
  e.g. General Practice, hospital in-patients, specialist clinics
❏ How do we measure the disease?
❏ How can we best measure response to treatments?
❏ How long should we (i) treat and (ii) study patients?
❏ How much of the test drug should we give?
  e.g. dose, frequency and duration of treatment
❏ What should we compare it with?
❏ What safety tests should we employ?
❏ What do the regulatory authorities permit/require?
❏ How should we analyse the results?

From this list alone you can see that a lot of specialist advice from doctors and nurses in the appropriate disease area, potential investigators, pharmacists, technical and laboratory staff, statisticians and regulatory affairs personnel will be required.

The designer must obtain all this information, collate it and then draft a trial protocol which is a detailed design document. The protocol should be agreed upon by all the contributors and formally approved by the drug company, investigator, ethics committee and regulatory authority.

What are the common drug trial designs?

The preferred experimental design for assessing efficacy and safety of a new drug is the randomised controlled trial (**RCT**). The most usual type of RCT for drug trials is the **group comparison**, in which patients are randomly allocated to either of two or more different groups which receive different treatments and the responses of each group are then compared.

Alternatively, you can compare the effect of one treatment after another on the same individual, and these are called **cross-over trials**. These trials only involve half the number of patients overall, but each patient is studied for twice as long as in a group comparison.

Sensible researchers often do a **pilot study** before the clinical trial begins. As the name suggests, this is a mini-study involving limited numbers of patients. The objective is usually to ensure that the chosen design, patient selection and trial procedures are feasible.

How are trials controlled?

Ideally, to test a new treatment in a group of patients, all other aspects of patient management should be **controlled**. If factors such as exercise, diet, medications other than the trial drug, etc. could influence the progress of the disease, they should, if possible, be the same for all patients in a trial. The people receiving the new drug are called the experimental group and the others are the control group. There are two common controls in drug trials - an 'active' control of another established or reference drug and an 'inactive' control, usually **placebo.**

This is an inactive substance (often chalk or lactose) which is made up to match the test drug, either as a tablet, capsule, injection or even as an inhaled or cream preparation. Considerable improvements are often seen in patients 'treated' with placebos. This is called **placebo response** and can be a major problem to drug companies who usually have to prove that a new drug is better than placebo. Sometimes one-third, or even half of the patients will respond adequately to placebos depending on the disease and psychological factors. Some patients do well without active drug treatment, possibly due to the disease being of short duration or even due to the effect of seeing their doctor or nurse more regularly and receiving extra attention, which is inevitably the case when patients are involved in clinical trials. This is particularly common in the elderly, perhaps isolated, patients, and in those with psychiatric problems. Unfortunately, you cannot predict which patients will do well on placebo. In some, e.g. life-threatening conditions, it can be very difficult or even unethical to employ a placebo control and doctors must exercise particular care in monitoring patients in these trials, often withdrawing them if they are at risk. Most regulatory authorities, however, require that Sponsors demonstrate absolute evidence of efficacy, compared with placebo, for a new treatment except in exceptional circumstances.

How many patients should be involved?

To have a complete understanding of the usefulness of a new drug, it might be ideal to give it to all the people suffering from the disease or condition which the drug is intending to treat. This would mean treating the whole **patient population.** Of course, this is unlikely to be either feasible or even desirable. So you have to select a **sample** of the population which you hope is representative. If it is a good sample, you could reasonably expect the results of your trial to be relevant and applicable to the population. It is important, both ethically and scientifically, for the sample to be big enough to detect a true difference between two treatments (or treatment and placebo) that is of clinical importance. The measure of this ability to detect a real difference is called the **power** of the trial. If you know the difference between two treatments which would be clinically significant and the variability of patient response in advance, a statistician can calculate a suitable sample size for your trial.

How are patients allocated to treatment?

Clinical trials, like any experiment, need to avoid **bias.** Bias can be introduced by the doctor, who may have a preference for one treatment, or by the individual patient or even by the choice of design itself which could favour one treatment. The first way to avoid bias is to **randomise** patients onto one or other treatment so neither the doctor nor the patient can predict which treatments each patient will receive. In practice, the drugs are packed and numbered according to a random list and patients are then given the next available numbered pack when they enter the trial.

Whilst most investigators recruit suitable patients as they

present at the clinic, sometimes it is possible to collect a significant number of patients, who have a chronic disease, who all start the trial on the same day. These groups of patients are called **cohorts** (the implication of military precision is probably over-optimistic!).

Occasionally, it may be useful to evaluate patients' suitability for a trial over a few days or weeks. Some diseases such as asthma, angina and epilepsy may not be assessed adequately on one occasion, so the patients may be entered into a run-in phase while they, for example, complete a diary card to record the number of episodes of wheeze, chest pain or fits, and also learn about the measurement techniques prior to allocation to trial drug(s). Sometimes this time is used to reduce and stop other drug therapies which would interfere with the trial, and this is commonly termed a **washout.**

What is a blind trial?

Trials where everyone is aware of the treatment received by the patient are called **open**. Examples of these would be trials of surgical devices, contraceptives or any comparison where treatment cannot be matched, like radiotherapy compared with drug therapy in cancer patients.

Many clinical trials, however, test drugs which can be matched and the doctor and/or the patient are unaware which treatment is being given. These are called **blind** studies, either **single blind** or **double blind**. Blinding is another way to minimise bias.

It is quite difficult to match different drugs so that they not only look and taste identical, but can also be given with the same frequency. Sometimes it is impossible to match the drugs, e.g. a drug given by injection and one in tablet form, but you can still keep doctor and patients 'blind' by making up dummy injections and dummy tablets, each patient receiving either a dummy injection and an active tablet, or a dummy tablet and an active injection, according to a random allocation. This approach, not surprisingly, is called **double dummy**.

What is a protocol?

The protocol is the name given to the design document. It is quite complex and may take several months to develop and finalise. There are fairly strict guidelines (e.g. GCP) which dictate what they should contain and most companies have their own standard formats and internal approval procedures. The following is simply a list of headings:

Introduction and Rationale
Aims / Objectives
Trial Design
Schedule
Patient selection criteria
Trial medication details
Procedures
    Allocation to treatment
    Informed consent
    Clinical assessments
    Laboratory assessments
    Adverse events and emergencies
    Concomitant medication
    Trial documentation
    Patient withdrawals
Monitoring and Audit procedures
Trial commencement and termination criteria
Statistical analysis
Reporting and publication
Ethical and legal issues
References
Appendices (including Summary, CRFs)

A good protocol should be clearly indexed, not least because many different parties need to refer to it. It must be clear and understandable to the doctors and nurses conducting the trial, ethics committees and the regulatory authority giving approval, the CRA co-ordinating the project, pharmacists, statisticians and regulatory affairs personnel, strategy, planning and, possibly, marketing personnel from the company. The protocol may form the basis of contracts (between companies and sub-contractors, e.g. laboratories and clinicians) so it is undesirable to change it once approved. Protocols are also central to clinical trial regulation (as explained in Chapter 2) and any amendment results in a repetition of the approval process which is both time consuming and expensive.

Case Record Forms (CRFs)

CHAPTER 6

●●● ## What is a Case Record Form (CRF)?

At the end of a clinical trial, possibly several years of work, the only tangible product is a collection of pieces of paper called case record or case report forms. These are the forms on which all the information and results of the clinical trial are recorded. They are designed to match the protocol, be filled in by the investigator, checked by the CRA and the results put onto a computer for analysis. A common source of confusion is that CRF is also used as an abbreviation for case record folder which is a bound 'book' of individual forms, sufficient for one trial patient.

●●● ## How are they designed and produced?

Many CRFs are designed by the CRA responsible for a trial, although larger companies may have a separate department which both designs and produces them. It is a real skill to structure the questionnaire or form so that it not only collects all the necessary information but is easy to complete, unambiguous and convenient for entering the data into a computer. Those who, like the author, struggle with government tax return forms, will be familiar with the frustrations of completing a complex form. Consider how much worse it must be to complete a ten page CRF whilst maintaining a caring consultation with a severely ill patient. There is a great temptation to design the CRF primarily to suit the person who checks it and/or enters the data onto computer. However, if the form does not accommodate the doctor or patient completing it, the poor quality of information collected and the amount of errors and omissions can compromise the entire project. With the advent of word processing and 'desk top publishing' packages, form design has become easier to do in-house. Many CRAs and their secretaries can now

produce print-ready proofs. Again, a word of warning:
however smart they look, it is important to show draft
copies to the investigators and ask them to try the CRFs
with a few patients and scribble on them with red ink.
Doctors, like other mortals, thoroughly enjoy correcting
and editing your script!

These days CRFs are fairly standardised: they will
invariably include the following elements:

information and consent forms	)	
patient selection checklist	)	beginning of
patient medical history	)	trial only
medication records	)	
clinical and laboratory assessments	)	repeated at
adverse event forms	)	each visit

end of study / withdrawal forms

Whilst the majority of the information is usually
recorded by the investigator, many trials also include
patient self-assessment forms or diary cards and special
care is needed to ensure these are easy to complete.

Usually each form is identified by a number designating
each investigator or centre, the patient number and the
date of assessment; each will also be signed by the
investigator.

Once they have been drafted, commented on by
investigators and data entry staff/statisticians and
redrafted, CRFs are printed on **NCR** (**N**o **C**arbon
Required) paper and bound into books or folders.
Often these are colour coded and have smart outer
boards printed with flow charts and aide-mémoires for
the investigator and dividers between each visit. They
are also usually perforated for easy removal of individual
sheets from the folder. A secretary with a good eye for
colour co-ordination and design may contribute much
to this process. If the printing, collating and binding is
done in-house, it is a considerable labour of love,
although satisfying (particularly for a small study!) and
needs careful quality control.

What about electronic CRFs?

Data collection still currently employs handwritten completion of paper forms. However, there are a number of innovations which are being more widely adopted. Some sites and studies are adapted to entering data directly onto a computer and transmitting it straight to the company data management department. This is known as **Remote data entry** and is particularly suitable for studies wherein the majority of the results are computer-derived, e.g. laboratory tests. Document scanning technology is currently available which is good for identifying numerical data. Sometimes there are logistic problems, e.g. CRF monitoring and SDV, with these methods and traditionally investigators are unwilling to enter data onto computer themselves - unless it was part of their routine practice.

What happens to completed CRFs?

Once the investigator has completed the CRF, it is usually checked on site by the CRA and then brought back to the office. The investigator is given one copy and the originals are forwarded to the Data Management or Biometrics Department. The information on the CRFs will then be extracted by data entry staff, either manually or using a scanner, and entered onto a specially designed database ready for analysis. Usually automated checks on the data for consistency and against the protocol are carried out. The CRA retains a spare copy in case Data Management personnel identify any queries or omissions. These are answered or corrected by the investigator at the next monitoring visit. Once the database is complete, quality control checks are undertaken to pick up any errors and then the database is released for analysis.

Once the whole study is completed the original CRFs will be archived by a drug company for fifteen years, or the lifetime of the product. The investigator must retain a register of the identification of trial patients for 15 years after trial completion.

CHAPTER 7   # Trial Supplies

What do you need for a trial?

In addition to a protocol and CRFs you need sufficient quantities of the drugs to be investigated to treat all the trial patients for the agreed period. It may be necessary to provide equipment for measuring the disease process or treatment response and for taking biological samples (blood, urine, swabs, skin samples etc). Also you need to prepare a considerable number of documents for each investigator.

How do you obtain drug supplies?

Once drugs are marketed, obtaining supplies is relatively simple. With the appropriate authority you can order them from pharmaceutical wholesalers or direct from the manufacturing companies. When the drug is still in development, it is usually produced in smaller quantities and possibly is only available from a research pharmacy. If you wish to compare your drug with another and they are to be 'blind' it will be necessary to obtain, for instance, unmarked tablets or pure drug material from the other manufacturer. Often, the CRA is able to simply send an appropriate requisition form to their clinical trials pharmacist who then orders drugs in bulk, packs them in bottles or blister packs and labels them. In a smaller company you may have the challenge of preparing the randomisation list, ordering, packing and labelling your own supplies. This must all be supervised by a pharmacist in suitable facilities. The labelling of trial drugs is most important and there are strict guidelines for each country and variations for some hospitals and certain classes of drugs. Once they arrive, the drug supplies must be kept in a secure (usually cool) room until despatched to investigator centres. Careful records must be kept of stock and transport arrangements, and code-lists are prepared both for the investigator and company.

What about medical equipment?

It is quite common for the drug company sponsoring a drug trial to provide the necessary equipment. This may be because it is desirable to standardise equipment or measurement techniques or simply because an otherwise suitable investigating centre lacks the appropriate technology. Often it is a centrifuge (used for spinning blood samples) or a freezer for storing blood or urine samples. The former are often available from contract (central) pathology laboratories or specialist rental firms who provide a delivery, maintenance and collection service. If your trial involves electrocardiogram (ECG) or blood pressure measurements, several companies offer a service providing a variety of machines, (including 24-hour heart monitors) interpreting the results and providing brief reports on each patient.

If medical equipment is recalled and re-issued, it is sensible to arrange for a full service and a check on calibration before dispatch. You may get involved in purchasing and distributing large and sophisticated equipment for some trials. Often the technician or junior doctor who will use it lacks training and the responsibility for arranging suitable instruction may also fall on the CRA and their colleagues.

 ## Where shall we do the blood tests?

Since now it is common to undertake multi-centre studies, drug companies increasingly choose to employ a central pathology laboratory to perform all routine haematology or biochemistry safety tests on samples from every investigating centre. This makes the results easier to analyse because every local laboratory has slightly different methods and **normal ranges**. These central or contract laboratories usually produce, on request, individualised test request forms (for inclusion in the CRF) and sample collection kits (syringes, needles, swabs, storage tubes and post-paid containers). The samples are posted direct to the lab who send the analysis reports to the investigators and CRA within about 24hrs. Most investigators find this approach very convenient and hospital out-patients are saved a long wait at the hospital lab. Often the laboratory will provide all the results on disc, which saves much data entry time and may reduce costs.

What documents do you need?

When the study is started or 'initiated' a number of documents should be provided by the drug company:

❏ Indemnity statements (from the company to the doctor and institution). These explain that the company will take responsibility for any drug-related problems providing the doctor keeps to the agreed protocol.

❏ CV form. The doctor must provide a CV or complete a form describing his qualifications, experience, current position and workload.

❏ Investigator agreement or statement. In this document the doctor agrees to fulfil all his responsibilities and adhere to the protocol, enrolling and treating patients within an agreed schedule.

❏ Financial agreement/letter. This contains the terms and details of the money to be paid to the doctor or his hospital/research fund (often per patient).

❏ Protocol. Often this has a page for final signatures.

❏ Declaration of Helsinki.

❏ Compensation guidelines. (ABPI (1991) in the UK) These explain procedures and conditions for payment of compensation to patients.

❏ CRFs and informed consent forms. These will be numbered per patient and include information sheets for patients to read and consent forms for them to sign.

❏ Adverse (Drug) Event reporting forms.

❏ Trial register. A list for recording patients' names and hospital numbers against their trial numbers.

❏ Dispensing list / Drug Accountability form. Forms for recording dates when patients receive and return their trial drug supplies.

❏ Sealed code envelopes. Individual numbered envelopes which identify patients' treatments in a blind trial (for emergencies).

❏ Investigator brochure. A booklet concerning all previous work reported with the test drug from the chemistry and pharmacy and animal work to early human trials.

❏ Investigator responsibilities list or GCP guidelines or explanatory booklet (sometimes appended to protocol).

❏ Copy of regulatory approval to conduct the trial.

❏ Laboratory normal ranges (if a central laboratory is being employed).

All these will be available or generated in-house and are usually collated in an Investigator Trial File so they can be explained, assimilated and stored conveniently. The investigator must add to this long list a letter of approval from his ethics committee before the trial can start.

How do you account for trial supplies?

Trial drugs and documents are both important and valuable and therefore care should be taken not only in storing and transporting them but also in documenting the process. The amount of drug issued should equal the amount the patient takes plus unused drug returned. This is called drug accountability. Someone must ensure that exact records are kept at both the investigating site (receipt, dispensing and returns) and the drug company. You may have a separate department of pharmacists working on this full-time - or you may have a locked cool room and forms to complete within the trials department. Unused and date-expired drug supplies may need to be destroyed, in which case a certificate of incineration should be obtained. It is desirable to deliver and collect trial supplies in person and, failing this, by a reliable courier service - the normal postal system is not adequate. For international clinical trials much time can be spent obtaining import licences and making appropriate shipping arrangements - particularly for refrigerated drugs such as insulins. Some of the documents have legal significance so it may be useful to log them in and out. Finally, trial supplies may require considerable amounts of secure storage space, ideally with convenient access for the trials department staff, since most supplies need to be personalised.

Clinical Research Associates

CHAPTER 8

Who becomes a CRA?

CRAs, also called Clinical Trial Co-ordinators/Scientists/ Officers/ Executives or **Monitors** in different companies, are invariably graduates with a background in a biological science, e.g. zoology, pharmacology, biochemistry, pharmacy, **physiology**. They should be able to communicate very well, both verbally and in writing. They need to have very good personal skills, be good communicators, persuasive and people should enjoy meeting them. Very often this means they have considerable personal confidence and are quite mature interesting people. Obviously they must be bright and presentable because they are dealing with sophisticated professionals (doctors and medical scientists, as well as pharmacologists, hospital administrators, etc). Over the past ten years the job has become more controlled in terms of standardised procedures, so CRAs also need to be rather obsessive in checking CRFs and meticulous in formally reporting, for example, any adverse events which patients might experience.

Twenty years ago monitoring clinical trials for a drug company was a natural progression for a medical representative. These independent individuals were familiar with the medical profession and their company's range of drugs and were also used to travelling extensively. These days it is relatively unusual for a representative to become a CRA unless the company wants to do Phase IV (marketed drug) trials with a predominantly 'field-based' team of monitors. It is now more usual for companies to employ scientists with research or laboratory experience. Often a PhD is a requirement, certainly for some of the senior posts or for early development phases where there is more 'science' involved. A few companies will employ non-graduate nurses and technicians. These people, whilst often just as competent as the graduates, will probably need further qualifications for significant promotion in major companies. On occasions, secretaries working for a medical department have been sponsored to do a part-time degree and become CRAs. In some continental countries it is quite common to employ medically qualified CRAs. Career prospects for CRAs are good, with many progressing to project management and R&D manager positions. Others progress to QA, regulatory or strategy/development roles.

Most CRAs have an office in the medical or clinical research department of a company. Some CRAs work from home, either on a freelance basis or for one company. This arrangement obviously reduces travel and modern technology has improved the quality of communications between the medical department and these field-based staff.

What do they do?

Primarily the CRA is a co-ordinator and 'enabler' of drug trials. Twenty years ago most of this work was done by a company medical adviser who had many other responsibilities. Now there are about 2,000 CRAs in the UK alone. As research into drugs becomes more regulated and therefore expensive, drug companies cannot afford to develop drugs slowly or with poor quality data. The industry believes that a trial will be better organised, run more to schedule and produce better data if it is co-ordinated by CRAs. This is invariably correct, particularly with multicentre trials. The industry has been proved right. The priority for most doctors is to care for individual patients, and trials with complicated paperwork and numerous extra patient assessments run more smoothly with logistic support and encouragement.

The CRA may be involved in designing the study and preparing the protocol and case record forms. They will usually select suitable investigators and organise all the trial supplies and any necessary training/instruction on trial procedures at the investigating centre. They will assist the investigator in obtaining ethics committee approval and liaise with their regulatory colleagues who will apply for permission to conduct the trial. They will arrange any necessary laboratory tests and liaise with pharmacies about storing and dispensing the trial drugs. Most CRAs also negotiate and supervise payment for all aspects of the clinical trial and arrange any investigator 'contract' which their company imposes.

Once the trial is under way, the CRA visits the investigator on a regular basis, to help with any problem that may hinder the smooth progress of the trial and to ensure patients are being treated absolutely according to the protocol. This will mean checking every patient's details against the selection criteria and comparing their recorded assessments with agreed procedures. The CRA needs to find out if all safety tests have been carried out and the results considered carefully; that proper informed consent is obtained from every patient and that the correct amount of drug is administered. This may all seem to suggest that doctors are not competent - this is not so! However, protocols are very complex documents and it is very easy to overlook, for example, that the patient is taking another drug which might interact with the new (test) drug or perhaps has a history of disease which does not comply with the exact terms of the protocol, for example an old peptic ulcer which might exclude them from involvement with a new drug for rheumatism, many of which can cause stomach problems. The manufacturer or developer of a new drug is given permission to do only carefully controlled studies and is responsible for ensuring that unsuitable patients are not exposed to a new and unlicensed drug.

The CRA must also make sure that the trial runs to schedule - and this is possibly the greatest challenge. If you need to study 100 patients to draw conclusions from a trial, it is no good at all having 27 at the end of the period, however well-controlled or high quality the data.

The CRA's lifestyle is varied and usually hectic. Many of them are visiting hospitals or health centres up to three days a week, checking progress and data, and providing administrative support (writing reports, answering queries, arranging supplies etc) for the remainder. Some CRAs work only on one trial in one area of medicine or one geographical region. Others co-ordinate numerous different trials in many therapeutic areas in different countries, using different languages.

A competent CRA must maintain their therapeutic and clinical measurement expertise and many become extremely knowledgeable about their chosen field. Often as 'their' drug approaches the market they will have opportunities to write papers and give presentations, both in-house and at public conferences.

What challenges do they have?

The major challenge faced by CRAs is that their success depends primarily on the hard work of someone else - namely the investigator - who has a completely different set of priorities. A second problem - shared by CRAs and investigators - is that of the disappearing patient population. The number of patients suitable for a trial during the protocol-writing stage is apparently always reduced by a factor of ten once the supplies are delivered! (This has been called Lasagna's Law after a pessimistic, or perhaps experienced, American investigator).

Other problems CRAs experience relate to the different approaches to medicine, both diagnosis and treatment, in different parts of the world. Measurement techniques and even healthcare systems vary enormously. If they work for a Japanese or American company who send a fixed protocol over to Europe for a trial with British or French doctors, the CRA may have the utmost difficulty persuading investigators to participate in the trial. Similar issues are encountered with CRFs designed in a different culture or country.

CRAs who work with drugs in early phases of development may experience difficulties or delays in getting permission to conduct the trial, either from ethics committees or national regulatory authorities. It is usually easier when several hundred patients have been successfully treated without mishap. Also, in the early years, the long term stability of the drug may not yet be established, so CRAs may have to deal with deteriorating drug supplies and short shelf-lives.

Like other travelling people, the CRA is vulnerable to motorway jams, air traffic control delays and the other irritations which are the daily lot of executives on the move. Since their appointments are often squeezed in between theatre lists and ward rounds and therefore fairly inflexible, many CRAs experience a high degree of stress.

Who supports the CRA?

Probably the most important source of support for the CRA is their secretary or personal assistant. You can imagine that, being out of the office up to three days a week, they need to be confident that someone competent can handle queries and their administration in their absence and arrange their itinerary thoughtfully. A clinical trials secretary can become familiar with all the investigators, protocols and emergency procedures, and assist with supplies preparation and co-ordination. There should also be opportunities to organise joint investigator meetings and conferences. Many clinical trial secretaries have prior experience in the health service and have studied for the AMSPAR Diploma for Medical Secretaries.

Other technical support for the CRA is provided by medical advisors, pharmacists, information scientists, data management staff and statisticians. Drug development is a team exercise and project management skills are vital for a successful programme.

What is a CRO?

A **Contract Research Organisation** (CRO) is an independent company which undertakes (clinical) research projects on behalf of drug companies. They vary in size and expertise from the small data management or training companies run by a handful of people, to international organisations offering a complete drug development service to the highest standards. The rise in popularity of CROs has followed a harsher economic climate for the drug industry with many companies needing to reduce the number of permanent staff, whilst the regulations call for an increased workload per trial. Companies principally employ CROs to monitor, analyse and report trials when they have internal staff shortages or need to conduct trials in a country where they have no staff or experience. Most CROs operate to their own SOPs but interact very closely with the Sponsor medical management. Regulatory authorities (and GCP) accept that Sponsors may choose to delegate any or all of the clinical trial process to CROs, but emphasise that the Sponsor should ensure that the CRO has adequate facilities and competence.

A CRA working for a CRO will have a very varied life - often working in many different therapeutic areas, for several Sponsors. Sponsors understandably assume that they will be well-trained and experienced and the trials will all run on schedule. It is therefore a tough environment in which to begin a CRA career, but often an area of considerable opportunity in project management. Apart from the very large CROs, however, they are unlikely to be involved in the development of a drug from Phase I to the market.

Monitoring and Adverse Events

CHAPTER 9

Why monitor trials?

Thirty years ago the drug industry arranged their clinical trials rather informally. Supplies of new drugs were given to experienced doctors who tried them on a series of patients and pronounced on their usefulness. The trials were small and informal, documentation was minimal and the end product was often a paper published in a medical journal.

Now it is different. With increasing requirements for more and more information on new drugs before they are given a licence, drug development has become a much longer and more expensive process. Also, the paperwork involved in clinical trials is complex and time consuming. Generally speaking, the tasks you are reminded about and encouraged in get done more quickly than those no-one mentions. Doctors are no exception to this. Also, they are used to making independent, sophisticated decisions about diagnosis and treatment without reference to any textbook, so it is not always easy for them to adjust to following a protocol devoutly.

In both these areas the CRA can benefit the progress of the trial positively. A trial in which a skilled CRA is involved will invariably progress more quickly and with higher quality data than one in which the protocol and trial supplies are posted to a doctor without any follow up.

How do trials get started?

Once you have designed the protocol and CRFs and selected your investigators, there is a good deal of preparatory work before the trial can start.

Firstly, the protocol must be submitted to the ethics

committee for approval. In some cases a central ethics committee can be approached directly by the CRA. Local committees must be approached only by the investigator, although it is common for the CRA to complete the necessary paperwork. The chairman or secretary will confirm how many copies of the protocol and other documents are needed and the date of the meeting. If the drug is not licensed, the trial and investigator involvement must also be approved by the regulatory authority, e.g. the MCA. Details of this process can be found in Chapter 2.

Usually, whilst trial approvals are awaited, the CRA organises all the trial supplies. (Details of trial supplies are discussed in Chapter 7). All the papers which a doctor must sign and keep for reference must be made ready for the 'start up' or initiation meeting. At this meeting the CRA meets with the principal investigator to confirm all the final arrangements about the trial agreement (between Sponsor and investigator), including protocol, finance, indemnity or insurance. The CVs of investigators will be collected and all the trial supplies (drugs, documentation, CRFs and equipment) delivered and explained. The CRA will also meet with the pharmacist, research nurse and any other hospital or clinic staff who will be involved. The purpose is to ensure everyone understands what is required and their respective responsibilities. It is another opportunity for the CRA to answer any questions about the drug or the trial protocol, clarify the trial schedule and establish good communication links with the centre.

Once all the appropriate permissions have been obtained and necessary supplies arranged, the clinical trial can then be started. It is not unusual for the preparation to take 3-6 months, or even longer with International studies.

How are investigators 'monitored'?

CRAs monitor their trials primarily by supporting the investigator. The first step is to consult the doctors when designing the protocol and CRFs so that these are suitable for the type of patient and disease. If the requested tests and examinations are similar to normal medical practice the assessments are more likely to be correctly reported. The CRA's next role is to supply everything the doctor and his staff need to conduct the trial and explain it all: how to fill in the forms, where to send the lab samples, when to do each test etc. If the nurse or junior doctor will actually do the work, then the CRA must meet with them and provide all possible assistance. The CRA must ensure the investigator knows his legal and ethical responsibilities and agrees with every aspect of the clinical trial before it starts.

Once the trial is under way, the CRA will be in touch regularly by telephone and letter and will visit the investigator, usually every 4-6 weeks, to discuss progress. At these meetings any problems will be reviewed, solutions proposed and the investigator encouraged to give the trial priority. The CRA must check that patients are being enrolled into the trial correctly: for example, that patients of the correct age and disease severity are being recruited, and that no-one with **contra-indicated** (or disallowed) **concomitant medication** has been entered into the trial by mistake. They must also check for adverse events or inadequate clinical effect, abnormal lab test results or any other problems. The trial supplies should be checked to see they are being stored and dispensed properly.

These meetings (and telephone contacts) must be carefully reported and archived by the CRA as part of their monitoring role.

What is data monitoring?

An increasing part of the CRA's job is the checking of completed case record forms. When visiting the investigator the CRA may spend anything from thirty minutes to several hours reading through the CRFs looking for omissions, inconsistencies or illegible doctors' handwriting(!). This is sometimes called data validation. Before any CRF is collected all queries should have been corrected by the investigator. The CRA then usually brings the CRF back to the office, checks it again to make sure every page is complete and properly identified, and then passes it to the data-entry staff who enter all the information onto a computer database. Very often, at this stage, further queries are found and relayed back to the CRA, who must return to the investigator and request clarification.

You will appreciate that this exacting part of the trial is time consuming and sometimes very tedious. However, at the end of the trial the only product (apart from, hopefully, patients who have been helped) is a small mountain of coloured paper - or CRFs. You cannot have a high quality study without high quality data.

What is Source Data Verification (SDV)?

SDV is the process of checking the trial records or CRFs against the patient's hospital records or GP notes and any other original test results, to prove that the CRF is correct. CRAs must obtain permission to get access to these records. During monitoring visits the CRA then cross-checks, often together with the investigator, certain key information about the patient and their treatment. This process must be carefully recorded and any discrepancies rigorously pursued.

What is trial termination?

At the end of a trial all the CRFs and supplies are collected and the CRA ensures all the necessary payments have been made. The investigator is asked to sign a statement confirming that all the trial patients gave informed consent and that their trial records will be filed securely.

The report or publication will be discussed in principle at this final (trial closure or **close-down**) meeting. This may mark the end of a three or four year collaboration between CRA and investigator and ideally should be conducted in such a way that both parties will seek an early opportunity to work together again.

A trial may also be 'terminated' prematurely in the case of inadequate patient recruitment (maybe just at that centre) or if new information causes concerns about the safety or efficacy of the trial drug. Occasionally, the CRA is unhappy with some aspect of the investigator's conduct (e.g. incorrect data recording, inadequate patient monitoring) and may decide to stop the trial at that centre.

What happens when things go wrong?

Testing new medicines carries a number of risks: perhaps it doesn't work as well as expected and people don't get better, perhaps their condition deteriorates; perhaps they suffer undesirable or 'side-effects'.

Think of any drug and you can find a group of people who do not benefit from it or are allergic to it. Think of any drug and you can also think of its side-effects. What is acceptable to a patient will depend both on the seriousness of their disease and also on their individual susceptibility to that side-effect.

One problem in developing drugs is discovering whether an undesirable symptom or event experienced by the patient in a drug trial is truly related to the test drug or not. As a result, instead of side effects, people now tend to refer to **Adverse Events** which can include anything that happens to the patient from the beginning to the end of the trial without making any judgement about what caused it. A good understanding of normal physiology, the condition being treated, the drug administered and the timing of the event will often enable decisions to be made later about whether or not the drug was responsible.

The investigator is responsible for warning his patients about possible, known, undesirable effects of the trial drugs, and then checking at every visit or assessment for any adverse events. Any adverse events which do occur during a trial must be recorded carefully and reported to the drug company.

How are Adverse Events reported?

Every CRF will have an Adverse Events section which will guide the investigator to examine the patient or enquire whether they have had any problems since their last visit. The doctor then records the nature of any undesired symptoms, their duration, severity and seriousness. Often the doctor asks about symptoms right at the beginning of the trial to try to establish which symptoms or problems are present before the drug is given. This provides a 'background' for comparison if additional problems occur during the trial. It should be noted that many people complain of significant adverse events whilst receiving placebo.

If the doctor has any major concerns for the patient, the trial drug treatment should be stopped, and the patient's symptoms monitored carefully.

The CRA or medical advisor should be contacted if the doctor believes an adverse event is 'serious'. Adverse events classified as serious include life-threatening events and those resulting in or prolonging hospitalisation and death. Depending on the stage of drug development, the drug company will then report the adverse event on special forms provided by the regulatory authority. Investigators at other centres, and their ethics committees, also have to be informed. Sometimes **serious adverse events** or a death will result in a clinical trial being suspended or cancelled. It may be that the trial will continue but extra precautions or safety tests will be incorporated. The problems of anticipating and interpreting life-threatening adverse events are highlighted by the fact that for most modern drugs the incidence will be less than 1 in 20,000 patients and may not be discovered until after the drug has been marketed.

The investigator must have an emergency 'phone number where he can contact a medically qualified drug company employee and discuss any adverse event and subsequent patient care. The investigator must also have access to the codelist in a 'blind' trial so that, in an emergency, he can quickly establish which drug the patient is taking.

Some drugs are very dangerous when taken in 'overdose' so it is important that they are stored securely and dispensed carefully. Again, if a patient exceeds the dose of a trial drug, the investigator needs immediate access to advice and information, which should be available from the drug company.

What about the patient?

There have been several tragic episodes in the course of recent drug development wherein patients have suffered excessively whilst receiving new drugs on trial. The media are usually quick to expose any supposed error of judgement on the part of the manufacturer or researcher. These experiences have resulted in individual doctors and some health authorities refusing to participate in clinical trials with new drugs unless the manufacturer provides a comprehensive indemnity insurance cover. This confirms that, should a patient attempt to sue the doctor, the drug company will accept responsibility, providing there was no medical negligence and the protocol was followed properly.

CHAPTER 10 # Analysis & Reports

How are trial results analysed?

Once the trial and the CRFs are completed, and the database is considered complete, the trial then enters analysis phase, i.e. the figures are examined and interpreted.

It is hoped that analysis will enable conclusions to be drawn, and the trial to have a definite outcome. Examples would be: Drug A works better than Drug B, or Drug A and Drug B are equally effective but Drug B causes more side-effects. Sometimes a negative conclusion will be drawn, e.g. Drug A is no better than placebo or showed no benefit to the patients treated.

The trial findings are usually entered from the CRF directly into a computer - this is called **data entry** - and tables are made of all the data.

The trial patients are then described, e.g. 27 males and 33 females with an average age of 45 in Group 1, and 24 males and 36 females with an average age of 41 in Group 2. Similarly, duration and severity of disease and other relevant factors will be examined and described. Before you can compare the effects of the drugs on the groups of patients you must establish that each group was comparable at the beginning of the trial.

Once the patient's background information (or **demography**) is described you would look at the results for the various assessments made at each visit. Almost immediately the analysis can run into problems, for whilst every patient is likely to have an age and sex recorded, not everyone will have attended for every single assessment. When the data are being examined you have to decide what to do about the gaps - a patient could have missed a visit because he was ill, or missed the bus or felt he was cured. Similarly, patients drop out of trials for a variety of reasons: adverse events, because they felt their condition was worse on the test drug or no better, because they were 'cured' or perhaps because they didn't like the measurement techniques/the doctor's manner/the taste, etc. Sometimes you know why results are missing, more often you don't, and therefore you can't assume the results that day would be better, worse or the same as at the previous visit. Very often the analysis of why and how many patients withdrew from the trial can be the most important outcome of a trial of a new drug.

Once the patients are described and omissions have been established, the results of the trial can be considered. Usually the analysis is undertaken at the end of the study, after the blind code has been broken. On rare occasions, it may also be necessary to conduct an interim analysis at predetermined stages of the study.

What are statistics?

Statistics simply are the collection and organisation of numerical facts or data. The word derives from the Greek 'Statis', meaning the State, as originally statistics were figures collated for the State, e.g. in population census. They can help us describe numerically the findings of a clinical trial, both by summarising the data and also to establish the cause of the difference between the experimental and control groups.

A well-known descriptive statistic is the **mean** or average; another common way of describing the mid-point of a series of figures is the **median** which is literally the middle number if they were arranged in ascending order. The **mode** is the most frequently occurring number in a series. Another useful descriptive statistic is the range.

An example:
Supposing you wished to describe the ages of a small trial in 7 children; it would be usual to talk about an average and range:

Ages: 4   7   7   8   9   10   11   years
           Mean = 56 divided by 7 = 8
           Median = 8
           Mode = 7
           Range = 4 - 11

There are two possible explanations for a different level of response between two groups: it could arise by chance - perhaps because the two groups varied in composition or it could be because one treatment was different/better than the other. A statistical test is used to determine whether the results could have occurred by chance.

Depending on the actual trial design there are several ways of testing the results:

❏ compare the proportion of patients showing a particular response, e.g. 15/30 were cured in Group 1 at week 8 and 23/30 in Group 2.

❏ compare the average results, e.g. improvement, for each group.

❏ look at the difference between the pre-treatment and post-treatment measures for each patient, and compare these for each group.

Industry statisticians employ automated statistical packages to perform statistical tests on trial data which enable complex analysis to be performed very quickly.

Is the result significant?

When an experiment is conducted and a result obtained it is important to be able to interpret the relevance. In drug development you have to ask - "Is it of any **clinical significance**?" This decision is up to the clinician and has very little to do with statistics. However, any scientist also wishes to know "Could the result have happened by chance?" You would like to think that your clinical trial is conducted on a representative sample of the patient population, but it is necessarily a highly selected sample. Perhaps the same trial done with a different sample would produce a different result. It is usual to apply **significance tests** to your data to establish the **probability (p)** of the result being a chance finding. It is beyond the scope of this book to describe the different tests habitually employed for clinical trials data. However, when reading about clinical trials you will see the expression 'a **statistically significant** result' and this usually refers to a **p** value of less than 5% - which means less than a 5% likelihood of the result arising by chance.

How are reports prepared?

Clinical trial reports may be statistical or clinical - or an integration of both. Statistical reports describe the data, the analysis and the results of any significance tests applied to them. Clinical reports describe the clinical context and relevance of the results and discuss the wider implications, e.g. in comparison to other treatments, the importance of reported side-effects etc.

These reports are often, naturally, prepared by statisticians and medical advisors - either as part of the drug company or external contractors. Reports are also commonly prepared by CRAs and project leaders in clinical trial departments or regulatory affairs personnel. If the trial has been performed to provide evidence in support of a Product Licence it will be structured in a specific way to suit the Regulatory Authority. In addition, most companies have their own in-house style. Usually trial reports contain the following elements:

❏ Trial investigators and identification
❏ Introduction and Rationale
❏ Methods: Patient selection criteria, drugs, measurements (clinical and laboratory), statistical analysis
❏ Results: Demography, safety, efficacy, withdrawals etc.
❏ Discussion
❏ Conclusions
❏ Data tables (appended)

The final report should be signed by the author, investigators, statistician and responsible medical advisor for the company.

Although most reports are prepared after trial completion, for some long-term trials, this focuses on trial progress and any adverse events reported - without formal analysis. A brief annual report may be prepared for the regulatory authorities or ethics committee.

Interim reports may also be produced at certain key points in the trial, but this is unusual because it is considered undesirable to 'break the code' before all the patients have completed.

What about publication?

Most researchers, and drug companies, are keen to publicise encouraging results with their new drug. Very often junior doctors need a few published papers to enhance their promotion prospects. As a result, clinical trials with positive results are frequently published either as papers in medical journals or as verbal presentations at academic medical conferences.

Papers must be written in a specified style to suit the journal of choice. Prestigious journals such as Lancet and the British Medical Journal have expert editors who review papers for scientific interest and originality and may take many months to have a paper accepted and published. Some clinical trials are of more commercial than scientific merit and these may only find their way into print promptly if a 'paying' journal is approached. These have fewer editorial requirements and survive by printing drug trial reports.

Drug companies often favour holding a small symposium to discuss and publicise the development of a new drug. Medical opinion leaders are usually invited to hear a series of papers presented by investigators. These are later published as symposium 'proceedings'. In smaller companies these symposia may be arranged by the medical department staff once the Product Licence Application is submitted for the new drug. CRAs and medical secretaries may find themselves organising travel and venues as well as typing and proof-reading abstracts and papers for publication and preparing slides. Although time-consuming, these events may be the culmination of many years of hard work in clinical trials with the new drug and can be a satisfying and sociable way to finalise the programme.

CHAPTER 11

SOPs, Audits and Archives

What are Standard Operating Procedures (SOPs)?

A Standard Operating Procedure document is a step by step guide to the standard way routine processes or tasks are done in a company or clinical trials department. People have been writing down common procedures and instructions since script was invented, but SOPs have been specifically introduced by the drug regulatory authorities and industry for laboratory, manufacturing and research practices. The possession of SOPs for all your clinical trial activities is a vital requirement if you are to comply with GCP. As mentioned in Chapter 3, most companies need to achieve GCP standards so that authorities all over the world will accept and respect the quality of their drug research work.

You would normally have SOPs for such key activities as protocol writing, monitoring, adverse event reporting, drug accountability, data management, study analysis and reporting and archiving. Often companies have SOPs for many other activities as well.

Who needs them?

If the SOPs are written in a fluent and readable way, they can be a very helpful addition to your department's training material. If new members of staff join the department, let them read the SOPs and they will have an immediate idea not only of what is done, but by whom and how. Usually, comprehensive SOPs grow into mighty tomes which may be too daunting to read en bloc but which provide an ideal reference if you need to know specific information. This can be a great help for all those times when you only think of the question when there is no-one there to ask, or you have already asked ten things that morning and can't bring yourself to do it again! Complex SOPs usually have accompanying checklists or aide-mémoires which simplify matters.

So SOPs are useful to new staff, people who can't keep all the details of a complex job in their head, managers and finally the auditors or quality assurance staff. The latter have the job of reporting whether everyone is following the SOPs or simply 'doing their own thing'.

Why have clinical trial audit?

You will be accustomed to the accounts of a company being audited by an independent group who report on financial irregularities and generally on the way the books are kept. Audit of clinical trials has been introduced for the same reason. Just occasionally someone gets over-enthusiastic about the virtues of their drugs and rarely (but it still happens) someone cheats. It could happen that an investigator forgets to make some measurements and invents them later to keep the CRFs complete, or even that a CRA is negligent and doesn't report adverse events properly.

So it was deemed sensible to have some unbiased observer examining the records of a trial and reporting any deviation from the protocol or company SOPs. In addition to Quality Assurance staff, principally auditors, many companies also employ quality control staff to conduct ongoing compliance checks to ensure adherence to SOPs.

How will we be audited?

Most clinical trial audits are performed routinely at a pre-arranged date and in a predictable way - indeed, you should have an SOP for audits. The auditors will arrange to visit the department and will either request a particular set of archives to be made available, or will arrange an audit of an investigator at their clinic. They may wish to check drug accountability records, sample storage, laboratory procedures, monitoring or source data verification. Data management, the appropriate use of computers and reporting procedures should also be audited.

Whatever the subject, the auditors prepare a comprehensive report which is usually sent to the medical directors and senior managers. No-one enjoys 'being checked up on', but clinical trials audit may improve the safety of drug trials and certainly increases their acceptance by regulatory authorities. Auditors will often have helpful ideas about how to improve standards and procedures. Some companies have adopted a policy of auditing all their clinical trials, but frequently companies focus on just the core regulatory trials.

Occasionally, a company may have anxieties about the quality or validity of an investigator's data. They can request the company QA staff to conduct a thorough site-audit to provide an independent view of standards.

In some countries, the drug regulatory authority has a team of inspectors who conduct audits on investigators and drug companies' trial records. They will examine SOPs, cross-check the case record forms and trial reports against patient records and compile an extensive QA report. The FDA has been following this practice, throughout the world, for many years and European countries are now following their example.

Where shall we put this?

With the increasing emphasis on carefully documenting all trials activities, it is very important that filing and archiving is done well. Invariably, the filing is covered by an SOP, as it may become quite complex to decide when and where a document should be copied, filed or archived, particularly in a multinational company. The secretary or office manager should be responsible for creating and maintaining scrupulous files for all the medico-legal documents, correspondence, reports and patient data. Most companies keep these originals together in a **Trial Master File**. Most trial files will have the following subsections:

- ❏ originals of protocol and case record forms
- ❏ investigator details
- ❏ monitoring reports and correspondence
- ❏ finances
- ❏ drug accountability records
- ❏ adverse events
- ❏ code lists
- ❏ ethical and legal letters (e.g. approvals, indemnities, contracts)
- ❏ trial results and reports

Completed CRFs, queries and other original patient data such as lab reports are usually filed separately, often in fire-resistant containers. Certain documents must be retained for inspection as long as the drug is on the market, in case a regulatory authority raises questions (in the future) and then all the research data might need re-examining. Therefore, on trial completion, the CRFs and important trial documents must be archived carefully.

CHAPTER 12

Pharmaco-economics

Why is health economics important?

The cost of providing healthcare is rising - for a number of reasons. Firstly, we are getting older as a population, and living longer: by the year 2020 there will almost double the proportion of people aged over 65 compared to 1960 - and we need much more healthcare as we get older. Secondly, people in western society have high expectations for their own health, for a good quality of life and use of the latest and best technologies. All of these factors serve to increase the cost of providing healthcare. Drugs account for between 8 and 18% of the healthcare budget (depending on the country concerned). So governments, individual health authorities and doctors are keen to get the best value for money for their patients. In the absence of measures of quality and quantity of health gained by drug treatment, the cost may be the main criteria for choice.

Health economics provides mechanisms to measure the value of different healthcare treatments and technologies, to enable sound decisions to be made about allocating scarce resources.

There are ever increasing demands being made on drug companies to demonstrate that their new drugs are good value for money - sometimes at the time of registration and certainly when prices and reimbursement arrangements are being set. Pharmaco-economics is that sector of health economics which focuses on the economics of drug treatments.

Quality of Life

Quality of Life encompasses physical, social and emotional aspects of an individual's existence and attempts to describe how they function and derive satisfaction from life. If our Quality of Life is important, then we need to be able to measure the impact a new treatment may have on it. For example, an effective migraine drug may improve our Quality of Life dramatically, but a chemotherapy treatment for cancer may reduce our Quality of Life because of the grim adverse effects.

Measuring patients' Quality of Life provides a basis for improving treatment choices - not only for individual patients and doctors but also for drug companies and governments when they need to decide which drugs to develop or buy.

How is Quality of Life measured?

There are several different approaches to measurement of Quality of Life, from general questionnaires to disease-specific scales which focus on the particular impact which the disease symptoms have on individuals. One of the earliest scales focused on two dimensions - distress and disability. Another looks at the impact of sickness on Activities of Daily Living (**ADL**) and behaviour in 12 different categories. Some researchers also use **Health Status** scales which attempt to measure an individual's level of functioning in terms of physical, social and mental wellbeing.

One of the problems for using Quality of Life measures in clinical trials has been the lack of agreement about which scale to use. Many experts have attempted to overcome this by developing a scale which has been validated in different cultures and diseases - the EUROQOL scale.

Quality of Life measures are often now employed in late phase clinical trials. Their inclusion may provide helpful additional information. This may be offset by the logistic challenge - not all investigators have experience in using these scales and some questionnaires are very time-consuming for both patient and doctor/nurse.

By using interviews and focus groups, researchers have been able to measure patients' preferences for certain disease states - on a scale on which 1 = healthy and 0 = dead. These measures are used in economic evaluations to derive values or utilities such as Quality Adjusted Life

Years (**QALYs**) - a measure of quantity (i.e. length) and quality of life. These measures enable costs and Quality of Life to be combined and then compared for different diseases.

What is economic evaluation?

Economic evaluation is simply a means of measuring the health resource implications of alternative treatments and management systems by considering the various healthcare 'inputs' (e.g. drugs, doctor's time, hospital beds) and consequences (e.g. improvement in health or avoidance of an undesirable event such as a heart attack). Economic evaluations vary in their perspective: they may aim to reflect the viewpoint of society, which would involve healthcare, social services and family inputs together with health and financial consequences and impacts on productivity. Alternatively, an evaluation may take a particular healthcare perspective looking at costs and consequences for the hospital sector and not considering the effect on social services resources or patients' own costs. All economic evaluations involve measuring the inputs and the outcomes and then giving each a value, for two or more competing treatments.

The most common form of economic evaluation today is **cost-effectiveness** analysis in which the outcome or effect of two treatments may vary but can be measured in the same units, e.g. number of infections resolved (by antibiotics), and the costs are then compared as cost per unit outcome, e.g. cost per infection resolved. If the outcome of different treatments proves to be the same, only the costs need to be considered and this is then called a **cost-minimisation** analysis - the aim being to decide the cheapest treatment. **Cost-benefit analysis** is used when both inputs and outcomes of different treatments can be expressed in financial terms. **Cost-utility analysis** is used when the treatments to be compared have different outcomes in terms of quantity and quality of life. These studies measure the amount of 'utility' or value derived from the treatment by the patient - often using QALYs, and this type of analysis compares two treatments' cost per QALY. This form of economic evaluation is very useful when, for example, a health authority must decide on which patients to spend scarce resources (or money). Perhaps they want to know whether heart transplants or kidney dialysis provide the best value for money for the local population. A cost-utility analysis can help decide priorities based on the cost per QALY of each treatment. Finally, **cost-of-illness** studies describe the total cost or economic burden of a particular disease to society. They include the direct costs for the healthcare system, community services and the family, the indirect costs such as productivity losses to the employer and family and, if possible, the intangible costs of pain and suffering. Although cost-of-illness studies are not complete economic evaluations, they can be useful in assessing the relative importance of a particular disease.

● ● ● ## Economic Analysis and Clinical Trials

Frequently, pharmaceutical companies are including an economic evaluation in their development plan, sometimes as part of the Phase III and Phase IV studies. Whereas randomised clinical trials are designed to test efficacy and safety, there are a few problems in using them to predict the costs and general effectiveness of a treatment once it is being prescribed 'in the real world'. Clinical trials involve very careful monitoring of specially selected patients, often in the very best clinical environment. Trial patients are motivated to take their drugs carefully and have many extra safety tests. Often many of the visits and tests would not happen in normal clinical practice, so clinical trial settings tend to produce increased use of healthcare resources (costs) and also better efficacy results. This necessarily artificial set-up is not ideal for economic analysis.

As a result, companies need to consider more observational studies in Phase IV where a broader group of patients are treated with the new treatment and followed up in a more natural way. Methodologies for economic analysis alongside clinical trials are currently being developed both in industry and academia. Outcomes research, which encompasses clinical, economic and social outcomes of treatments, is likely to become a growth area within pharmaceutical companies over the next few years.

Glossary  (of abbreviations and terms)

Glossary of Abbreviations

ABPI - The Association of the British Pharmaceutical Industry

ACRPI - Association for Clinical Research in the Pharmaceutical Industry

ADE - Adverse Drug Event

ADL - Activities of Daily Living

ADR - Adverse Drug Reaction

AE - Adverse Event

AICRC - Association of Independent Clinical Research Contractors

BP - British Pharmacopoeia

CPMP - Committee for Proprietary Medicinal Products

CRA - Clinical Research Associate

CRF - Case Record Form, Case Report Form or Case Record Folder

CRO - Contract Research Organisation

CSM - Committee on Safety of Medicines

CTC - Clinical Trial Certificate

CTX - Clinical Trial Certificate Exemption

CV - Curriculum Vitae

EMEA - European Medicines Evaluation Agency

FDA - Food and Drug Administration (US regulatory authority)

GCP - Good Clinical Practice (sometimes called Good Clinical Research Practice)

GLP - Good Laboratory Practice

GMP - Good Manufacturing Practice

ICH - International Conference on Harmonisation

IND - Notice of Claimed Investigational Exemption for a New Drug

IRB - Institutional Review Board (Ethics Committee)

MCA - Medicines Control Agency

NCE - New Chemical Entity

PLA - Product Licence Application

PMS - Post Marketing Surveillance

QALY - Quality Adjusted Life Year

QoL - Quality of Life

RCT - Randomised Controlled Trial

SDV - Source Data Verification

SHO - Senior House Officer

SOP - Standard Operating Procedure

SR - Senior Registrar

TMF - Trial Master File

(Abbreviations of common medical qualifications and how to use them can be found under Further reading/ Resource material)

Glossary of Terms

Adverse drug reaction (ADR) - adverse events that are considered to be caused by a trial drug.

Adverse event - any undesirable experience (occurring during a clinical trial), whether or not it is considered to be drug related. (See also Serious Adverse Event)

Analogues - drugs which are similar or come from the same family.

Animal models - artificially created animal preparations which mimic a medical condition, designed to test the effects of new drugs.

Audit (of a trial) - a comparison of source data and associated records with the Trial Report to determine whether the trial has been accurately reported. In addition, an audit should check whether the trial was carried out in accordance with the protocol and the SOPs.

Bias - an opinion, feeling or influence that strongly favours one aspect (or treatment) when there is a choice (treatment bias may be exhibited by doctors or patients, or both).

Black List (of investigators) - a list of investigators compiled by a company or Regulatory Authority whose data are not deemed acceptable and who will not be invited to collaborate in clinical trials. The FDA produce a list of investigators who have been 'blacklisted'.

Blind - a term used to describe a trial in which the patient or the investigator (and sometimes both) do not know what trial medication is being taken by the patient. (See Single Blind and Double Blind)

Carcinogenicity - potential to cause cancer.

Case Record Form, Case Report Form or Case Record Folder - a document which reflects the protocol and provides for the recording of all trial data for an individual subject.

Clinical significance - describes a result from a trial which is of clinical relevance.

Close down - the act of terminating a trial. Sites may be closed down because the trial has been completed or for safety or procedural reasons.

Concomitant medication - drugs (excluding the trial drugs) being taken by a patient during a clinical trial. They may have been prescribed for a different condition.

Contra-indicated - a term used in relation to treatments which are not permitted (during a clinical trial). Certain drugs are contra-indicated for subgroups of patients for reasons of safety.

Contract Research Organisation (CRO) - an institution or company (commercial or academic) to which a drug company may transfer some responsibility of the drug development process, e.g. trial monitoring, data analysis.

Controlled trial - in which groups of patients are managed in an identical manner with the exception of treatment received, and the responses are compared.

Cost-benefit - an analysis performed when both the inputs and outcomes of different treatments can be expressed in monetary terms and compared.

Cost-effectiveness - an analysis performed when the outcomes of treatments can be measured in the same units. Treatments are compared in terms of cost per unit outcome.

Cost-minimisation - an analysis performed when the outcome of two treatments is the same and which aims to decide the cheapest way of achieving that outcome.

Cost-of-illness - a descriptive study which itemises, values and sums the costs of a particular disease to provide an estimate of its economic burden.

Cost-utility - an analysis under taken when the outcomes of treatments differ in quantity and quality of life and are measured in utilities (e.g. QALYs). Treatments are compared in terms of cost per QALY gained.

Cross-over trial - in which individual patients receive both treatments one after another and their responses are compared.

Data entry - the process of transcribing the contents of a CRF onto a computer database for the purpose of analysis.

Demography - a description of the features of the trial population: their racial and physical characteristics, age patterns, disease history, etc.

Double blind - a term used to describe a trial in which neither the assessor (usually the doctor) nor the patient are aware of which treatment has been allocated.

Double dummy - a procedure for achieving blindness when comparing two unlike drugs wherein e.g. an active injection and placebo tablet are given to one group and the matching placebo injection and active tablet are given to the other group.

Ethics committee - an independent body, including medical and non-medical members who consider clinical trials in the context of safety, integrity and human rights.

Expert report - a report required by the Regulatory Authorities regarding some aspect of a drug (e.g. Toxicology, Chemistry and Pharmacy, Clinical). The author of such a report must be an expert in that particular field and may be a company employee or an external person.

Good Clinical Practice - a standard by which clinical trials are designed, implemented and reported so that there is public assurance that the data are credible, and that the rights, integrity and confidentiality of subjects are protected.

Group comparison - a trial design in which patients are randomly allocated to either of two or more treatment groups and the responses of each group are compared.

Health Status - the level of individual function in terms of physical, social and mental wellbeing.

Investigator - a medically qualified person responsible for the practical performance of a trial and for the welfare of the patient.

Investigator brochure - a booklet of all the relevant information known prior to the onset of a clinical trial including: chemical and pharmaceutical data, toxicological and pharmacological data in animals and the results of earlier clinical trials. There should be adequate data to justify the nature, scale and duration of the clinical study. The brochure should be updated during the course of drug development.

Indication - condition or disease which a drug is intended to treat.

Mean - the arithmetic average which is obtained by dividing the sum of the measurements by the number of measurements.

Median - the middle number when all the measurements are arranged in rank order.

Mode - the most frequently occurring value.

Monitor - a person appointed by the sponsor or Contract Research Organisation (CRO) who is responsible to the sponsor (or CRO) for the monitoring and reporting on the progress of the trial and for verification of data. The monitor must have the qualifications and the experience to enable a knowledgeable supervision of a clinical trial. Trained technical assistants may help the monitor in the collection of documentation and subsequent processing.

Multicentre trial - a clinical trial conducted according to one protocol, but in several different locations and therefore involving different investigators.

Named patient basis - an unlicensed drug being supplied to a doctor for use in a particular patient. The drug supply cannot be used for any other patient. The patient should be monitored carefully and a brief report supplied to the drug company.

Normal range - the range of values for a specific (usually laboratory) parameter which are considered clinically normal. These will vary slightly depending on the laboratory and are used as a reference against which individual patients' results are compared.

Open - a term used to describe a trial in which both the patient and the assessor are aware of the treatment being allocated.

Patient population - relating to patients: the total number of people suffering from a particular condition or disease.

Pharmacology - the science of the properties of drugs and their effects on the body.

Pharmacokinetics - study of the time course of absorption, distribution, metabolism and excretion of drugs by the body.

Phase I - first trials of a new drug in man, usually conducted in healthy volunteers.

Phase II - early efficacy and safety trials conducted in limited numbers of patients. They include dose-finding studies to establish an appropriate range of doses.

Phase III - major efficacy and safety trials in large numbers of patients. Ideally the circumstances of the trials should be close to normal conditions of use for the new drug.

Phase IV - trials performed after marketing of the drug, in indications for which it is licensed.

Physiology - the scientific study of the functioning of the body and all constituent systems.

Pilot study - a mini-study conducted in advance of the main experiment, usually to assess feasibility.

Placebo - an inert substance, with no pharmacological activity which is made up to look like a medicine. It is ineffective but may help the patient's condition because they have faith in its powers. New drugs are tested against placebos in clinical trials.

Placebo response - a patient's clinical response whilst receiving placebo treatment.

Post Marketing Surveillance - large Phase IV studies conducted to evaluate further the safety profile of a new drug, after a Product Licence has been granted.

Power - the likelihood that a trial design will be able to detect a real difference, when it exists.

Preclinical - referring to (research) activities prior to research in patients.

Probability(p) - the likelihood (e.g. of £ 5%) that an observed difference could have arisen by chance.

Protocol - a document which states the rationale, objectives, design and methodology of the trial, with the conditions under which it is to be performed and managed.

Randomise - relating to allocation of patients to a treatment: the process which ensures that each patient is allocated to different treatments in an unpredictable manner.

Regulatory authority - a government body, consisting of scientific experts and administrators who control the use of medicines and research on new drugs.

Remote data entry - direct, electronic transmission of clinical trial data from the investigator site to the Sponsor.

Run-in - a period at the beginning of a clinical trial during which no active trial drug is provided, often used to reduce (effects of) previous treatments, or to establish baseline severity of illness/eligibility for the trial.

Sample - a sub-group or selection of patients which should be representative of the patient population.

Scale-up - expansion of the manufacturing process of a new drug from research sized batches to commercial production.

Serious adverse event - an adverse experience that is fatal, life-threatening, disabling or which results in patient hospitalisation or prolongation of hospitalisation. In addition, congenital anomaly and occurrence of malignancy are always considered serious adverse events.

Significance tests - tests applied to a set of data which seek to establish whether the results could have occurred by chance and therefore their 'significance'.

Single blind - a term used to describe a trial in which either the assessor (usually the doctor) or the patient, but not both, are aware of which treatment has been allocated.

Statistical significance - statistical test result in which p is less than or equal to 0.05 (i.e. a 5% probability of the result occurring by chance).

Teratology - the study of developmental abnormalities and their cause.

Toxicology - the study of poisons, e.g. drugs, and their effects (on plants) and animals.

Toxicity - the degree to which a substance is poisonous.

Trial master file - a file or archive containing all the key documents as defined by GCP guidelines.

Washout - a treatment-free period either at the outset of a clinical trial or between two treatments of a cross-over trial. The purpose is to remove the effects of the previous treatment or avoid drug interactions.

Questions for Group Discussion

Chapters 1 - 3

❑ What are the different sources of new drugs?

❑ Why do we do trials in healthy volunteers?

❑ What is the role of a regulatory authority?

❑ What do ethics committees do?

❑ Describe informed consent and how it should be obtained?

❑ Why have drug companies adopted GCP?

Chapters 4 - 7

❑ How would you select an investigator?

❑ Why do doctors become investigators?

❑ What is the power of a clinical trial?

❑ Why do we use placebos in drug trials?

❑ What is a double dummy design?

❑ What is a pilot study and why would one be conducted?

❑ Who should be consulted when CRFs are designed?

❑ What are the key elements of a CRF?

❏ What are the advantages of a central pathology lab for a multicentre trial?

❏ What is an investigator brochure?

Chapters 8 - 12

❏ What personal attributes does a good CRA need?

❏ What are a CRA's principal responsibilities?

❏ What should trial monitoring achieve?

❏ What happens at an initiation meeting?

❏ Why is SDV performed?

❏ What are significance tests?

❏ Why are SOPs needed for clinical trials?

❏ Why are clinical trials audited?

❏ What are the benefits of Quality of Life measurement?

❏ Why have health economics become important?

Further Reading/ Resource Material

 ## Guidelines

ABPI (1991), Clinical trials - Compensation for medicine-induced injury

ABPI (1992), Code of practice for the clinical assessment of licensed medicinal products in general practice

ABPI (1992), Fraud and Malpractice in the context of clinical research

ABPI (1994) Relationship between the medical profession and the Pharmaceutical Industry

Department of Health (1991), Local Research Ethics Committees

International Conference on Harmonisation (1996), Good Clinical Practice: Consolidated Guidelines of Technical Requirements for Registration of Pharmaceuticals for Human Use (ICH ENGE 6)

Royal College of Physicians of London (1990), Guidelines on the Practice of Ethics Committees in Medical Research

Royal College of Physicians of London (1990), Research involving Patients

World Medical Association (1989), Declaration of Helsinki (Hong Kong Amendment)

Books

ABPI Data Sheet Compendium (A comprehensive list, per company, of prescribing information on drugs marketed in the UK)

Altman DG & Gore SM (1982), Statistics in Practice: Articles from the British Medical Journal, British Medical Association, London

British National Formulary, BMA & Royal Pharmaceutical Society (A manual listing details of all marketed drugs available in the UK, arranged according to therapeutic area, published regularly)

The Medical Directory, Churchill Livingstone/Cartermill Publishing (A three volume directory of UK doctors, published annually)

Jefferson T, Demicheli V, Mugford M (1996), Elementary Economic Evaluation in Health Care, BMJ Publishing Group

Lloyd J, Raven A (Eds) (1994), ACRPI Handbook of Clinical Research. Churchill Medical Communications (A comprehensive textbook on clinical drug development, written primarily for CRAs)

Lock S & Wells F (1993), Fraud and Misconduct in Medical Research, BMJ Publishing Group, London

Pocock S (1983), Clinical Trials - a Practical Approach, John Wiley, Chichester

Sneader W (1986), Drug Development: from laboratory to clinic, John Wiley (A concise paperback describing the breadth of the drug development process)

Spilker B (1991), Guide to Clinical Trials, Raven Press, New York

Winslade J & Hutchinson DR (1992), Dictionary of Clinical Research, Brookwood Medical Publications Ltd

Associations

Association for Clinical Research in the Pharmaceutical Industry (This is an association primarily for CRAs and study site co-ordinators. It has a regular journal, publishes educational material and provides information on CRA careers. Also there are conferences and workshops organised regularly.)
Judi Reader, ACRPI,
P O Box 1208, Maidenhead, Berks SL6 2YH.
(Tel: 01628-29617)

Association of Clinical Data Management (ACDM)
P O Box 1208, Maidenhead, Berks SL6 2YH.
(Tel: 01628-789450)

Association of the British Pharmaceutical Industry (ABPI)
12 Whitehall, London, SW1A 2DY
(Tel: 0171-930-3477)

Association of Independent Clinical Research Contractors (AICRC)
Department of Pharmacology and Therapeutics, University of Wales College of Medicine, Heath Park, Cardiff CF4 4XN
(Tel: 01222-747747 Ext 2353)

Association of Medical Secretaries, Personal Assistants and Receptionists (AMSPAR) (Professional association for a range of administrative staff working in the field; several courses and qualifications are available)
Tavistock House North, Tavistock Square, London WC1H 9LN
(Tel: 0171-387-6005)

International Conference on Harmonisation, ICH Secretariat,
c/o IFPMA, 30 rue de St-Jean, PO Box 9, 1211, Geneva 18, Switzerland
(Tel: 00 41 (22) 340 1200)

Society of Pharmaceutical Medicine
1, Wimpole Street, London W1M 8AE
(Tel: 0171-491-8610)

Statisticians in the Pharmaceutical Industry (PSI)
Mrs Carol McKellar, PO Box 37, Ely, Cambs CB6 3XY (Tel: 01353-648740)

The British Institute of Regulatory Affairs (BIRA)
34, Dover Street, London, W1X 3RA
(Tel: 0171-499-2797)

USE OF MEDICAL QUALIFICATIONS IN THE UK

The guidelines for adding letters after a name in formal medical correspondence are as follows:

1. Honours and decorations come before university degrees and diplomas:
    Sir Adam Haig, KBE, FRCS, or
    Adam Haig Esq., OBE, FRCS

2. Medical degrees are placed before surgical:
    Adam Haig, Esq., MD, FRCS

3. Surgical degrees take precedence over degrees in obstetrics and gynaecology:
    Adam Haig, Esq., FRCS, FRCOG

    A surgeon's MD should always be featured in his degrees

4. When postgraduate degrees are held, qualifying degrees may be omitted, e.g. Mr J Dunn, FRCS (omitting his qualifying degree of MB, ChB)

    Once MD qualification awarded, qualifying degrees are omitted, e.g. J Dunn MD FRCS and not J Dunn MB ChB MD FRCOG

5. University degrees take precedence over the qualifications of the Royal Colleges, which precede diplomas, e.g. Mr J Dunn, MB, ChB, MSc, FRCS, DMR

Although 'Esquire' has more or less been dropped in the commercial world, it is recommended as a useful term to be used when writing to the medical profession.

COMMONLY USED QUALIFICATIONS

BAO	Bachelor of the Art of Obstetrics
BCh/BChir/BS/ChB	Bachelor of Surgery
BM	Bachelor of Medicine
BSc	Bachelor of Science
CM, ChM	Master of Surgery
DCh	Doctor of Surgery
Dip.Pharm.Med	Diploma in Pharmaceutical Medicine
DM	Doctor of Medicine
DObst RCOG	Diploma in Obstetrics of the Royal College of Obstetricians and Gynaecologists
DPhysMed	Diploma in Physical Medicine
FRCGP	Fellow of Royal College of General Practitioners
FRCOG	Fellow of Royal College of Obstetricians and Gynaecologists
FRCP	Fellow of Royal College of Physicians of London
FRCPE*	Fellow of Royal College of Physicians of Edinburgh
FRCPGlasg.	Fellow of Royal College of Physicians and Surgeons of Glasgow
FRCPath	Fellow of Royal College of Pathologists

FRCPsych	Fellow of Royal College of Psychiatrists
FRCS	Fellow of Royal College of Surgeons
FRCSE*	Fellow of Royal College of Surgeons of Edinburgh
FRS	Fellow of Royal Society
LMS	Licentiate in Medicine and Surgery
LMSSA	Licentiate in Medicine and Surgery, Society of Apothecaries
LRCP	Licentiate of Royal College of Physicians
MAO	Master of the Art of Obstetrics
MB	Bachelor of Medicine
MC/MCh/MChir	Master of Surgery
MCh/Orth	Master of Orthopaedic Surgery
MD	Doctor of Medicine
MRCGP	Member of Royal College of General Practitioners
MRCOG	Member of Royal College of Obstetricians and Gynaecologists
MRCP Ed.	Member of Royal College of Physicians and Surgeons of Edinburgh
MRCP Glasg.	Member of Royal College of Physicians and Surgeons of Glasgow

MRCP (UK)	Member of Royal College of Physicians
MRCPath	Member of Royal College of Pathologists
MRCPsych	Member of Royal College of Psychiatrists
MRCS	Member of Royal College of Surgeons
MS	Master of Surgery

* This may be written as FRCP(Ed.), FRCP.Ed, FRCP(Edin.) or FRCPE. It is correct to add the appropriate college after the MRCP, FRCP or FRCS of the Scottish Royal Colleges.

Beyond What is Written

A Researcher's Guide to Good Clinical Practice

Ann Raven 1998. 92 pages. £10.50 ISBN 0 9517396 2 X

Written specifically for the researcher, whether doctor, nurse, pharmacist, principal investigator or study site co-ordinator, **Beyond What is Written** provides an accessible but comprehensive summary of the latest guidelines with respect to Good Clinical Practice, together with an introduction to ethics review procedures and Good Laboratory Practice.

ACTION HEALTH receives 10% of all sales of this book

Beyond What is Written

A Researcher's Guide to Good Clinical Practice

By Ann Raven

CONTENTS

Clinical Trial Design ▪ Patient Recruitment and Management ▪ Research Funders and Clinical Trials ▪ Ethical and Legal Regulation of Clinical Trials ▪ Good Clinical Practice ▪ Protocols and Investigator Brochures ▪ Management of Trial Supplies and Documents ▪ Case Report Form Design and Management ▪ Adverse Events in Clinical Trials ▪ Reporting and Disseminating Results ▪ Trial Management and Audit ▪ Laboratories and Good Laboratory Practice

"Successful clinical research is a true partnership between a sponsor and one or more clinical investigators. The sponsor and investigator hold joint responsibility for the science, ethics and quality of any research. Ann Raven's new book primarily addresses the basics of clinical trial methodology (including the relatively new area of outcomes research) and the processes required for Good Clinical Practice.

"Beyond What is Written... A Researcher's Guide to Good Clinical Practice" is an important addition to the literature of clinical trials. The book provides important background reading and reference material for researchers in clinical medicine who regularly or occasionally work on clinical trials as well as those who wish to do so in the future. It will enhance the way that clinical investigators understand the needs and requirements of their industrial and public sector sponsors, and in that way lead to increased efficiency and standards in clinical research."

Dr Mike Emanuel

Order Form

Please send me

Qty   Value

.... Consider it Pure Joy...   ....
           [An Introduction to Clinical Trials]
           @ £9.50 each

.... Beyond What is Written   ....
           [A Researcher's Guide]
           @ £10.50 each

10% Discount for 20 copies   ....

Postage and Packing @ £1 per copy   ....

                         TOTAL

Cheques (sterling) should be made payable to
"Cambridge Healthcare Research".

Name and address for despatch:

....

....

.... Post Code............................

Cambridge Healthcare Research,
Publications Division,
The Old Institute, High Street, Coton,
Cambridge CB3 7PL, UK.
Tel: 01954-211189
Fax: 01954-211915

Books may also be ordered via our website:
http://www.cambridgehealthcare.co.uk